W9-DIA-708

100 MEDITATIONS

100 MEDITATIONS

Selections from
Unitarian Universalist Meditation Manuals

COLLECTED BY
KATHLEEN MONTGOMERY

SKINNER HOUSE BOOKS
BOSTON

Published by Skinner House Books, an imprint of the
Unitarian Universalist Association, 25 Beacon Street, Boston,
MA 02108-2800

Printed in Canada

Cover design: Suzanne Morgan   Text design: WordCrafters
ISBN 1-55896-403-7

Library of Congress Cataloging-in-Publication Data
100 meditations : selections from Unitarian Universalist meditation
manuals / collected by Kathleen Montgomery.
    p. cm.
  ISBN 1-55896-403-7 (alk. paper)
    1. Meditations. 2. Spiritual life–Unitarian Universalist churches–
Meditations. 3. Unitarian Universalist churches–Prayer-books and
devotions–English. I. Title: One hundred meditations.
II. Montgomery, Kathleen.
BX9855.064 2000
242–dc21

                                                            00-028536

5 4 3 2 1

03 02 01 00

Note: Yvonne Seon and Sara Moores Campbell now go by the
names Yvonne Seon-Wood and Sarah York. We have printed
their names here as they were when the pieces were originally published.

     Every effort has been made to obtain permission to
include each of these pieces. In some cases the author is
deceased and we have been unable to locate his/her estate.

Excerpt from *The Prophet* by Kahlil Gibran. Copyright 1923 by
Kahlil Gibran and renewed 1951 by Administrators CTA of
Kahlil Gibran Estate and Mary G. Gibran. Reprinted by per-
mission of Alfred A. Knopf, a Division of Random House, Inc.

For my family:
Matthew and Elizabeth
Tobin and Shadie
Cameron, Ian and Simon

TABLE OF CONTENTS

MORE HUMAN THAN OTHERWISE

FAULT LINE

IT TOUCHES US

DAY OF PROMISE

PREFACE

I have always loved windows, the way the view from them frames and limits what one sees.

When I was a child I used to lie on the bed in my room in Detroit and look out the back window. I'd see past a small backyard, unkempt; past the alley, rat-ridden; through a littered vacant lot; across a busy street (Vernor Highway); and to a gas station. To the side of it, and a bit beyond, was a huge and ancient pin oak. I loved that tree. It was all I ever saw, really, from my window. I watched that tree season in and season out. Bare, green, greener, red, brown, bare. Year after year. It was a crutch and a comfort and a talisman.

Now, decades later, my favorite view is from the window in my office at 25 Beacon Street in Boston. In the winter, in the late afternoon, the sun slants on the brick buildings on the far side of the Boston Common. The bricks turn pink, then rose, orange, deep red, and eventually gray. Sometimes, in the middle of a meeting, I ask the people gathered in my office to marvel with me at the grace and the astonishing beauty of the view. Sometimes they see exactly what I see and sometimes they look at another view altogether. And, sometimes, they're just puzzled at the interruption.

Those two views capture how I feel about the meditations in this book. Each captures some fresh view and say something about what the world offers, a tough or a gentle truth. Many of them offer a single, unforgettable image: a star, a concerto, a feisty waitress. All of them linger in the memory long after they've been read.

Both the Unitarians and the Universalists brought to their merger a long tradition of publishing meditation manuals. And since that merger of the Universalist Church of America and the American Unitarian Association in 1961, at least one such small and wonderful book has been published each year, more recently two each year.

This collection, gathered from the more than 1700 meditations published since the merger, was created with a specific audience in mind: a reader looking for comfort and challenge, perhaps not a Unitarian Universalist but someone open to our values and our theology. For that reason the selections are not *about* Unitarian Universalism but *of* it. Each is by a Unitarian Universalist; each, I think, captures something important embedded in our tradition.

The experience of reading and re-reading through almost forty years worth of these manuals was humbling; there are so many elegant, eloquent words. And there was discomfort too. There were no meditations by a woman until Mary Lou Thompson's collection, *Stopping Places,* in 1974. The earlier meditations were riddled with gender-specific language, though, with one or two exceptions, we have received permission to amend them as they appear here. Prior to Jacqui James' and Mark Morrison-Reed's collection, *Been In the Storm So Long,* in 1991, only one meditation by an African American had been published. The voices of other people of color are still absent. We have changed and we continue to change—but slowly, painfully slowly.

It's been a privilege to spend time with these past meditation manuals. And while I asked for and got a lot of opinions about which past meditations have been important to others, it has been challenging and rewarding to, finally, make my own choices about which would be reprinted here, which ones most touch my heart. This volume comes with my thanks to all those who offered advice and encouragement, to my colleagues in the UUA's publications office who creatively and patiently helped shape this handsome volume, and most particularly to the women and men whose voices and visions are included here, who generously share the views from their own windows.

KATHLEEN MONTGOMERY

BEAT OF LIFE

BEAT OF LIFE

If none will sing of life
Then I will sing its praise.
Not in the treble voice of youth,
Nor on instruments of one string,
Nor with happy, laughing brasses,
Nor by cadence counting on drums
Would I praise life, as those
Who sing hymns only to the sun,
Forgetting nature in torment,
Man in agony. I would sing
Soft and sad, surging with emotion,
Remembering pain, fear and death,
Those swamping morasses, and seed beds, too,
Where courage, life and growth
Began to bloom, and man in sweat
Quivered at what he saw, and
Spoke in verse, ballad and epic,
Recounting glory, learning self,
Hailing life as the deep surge to be,
Singing in deep voice the hymn
Which extols restless beings tense with destiny.

ARTHUR GRAHAM
PARTS AND PROPORTIONS, 1961

THE NEED TO BE STILL

Some of us with muscles and nerves singing in the
    full flush of youth,
Some with quiet confidence, and some perhaps
    weary,
Worn with the failures, the years, and the passing
    of strength,
And still others, the men and women determined,
Filled with the zeal of battle for justice yet to be
And for truth still denied or undiscovered—
Each and all of us, whatever we be,
Must come to the time when we need to be still.
There comes a time when we must know the need
To go apart and meditate, to seek the meanings
    of our lives,
To reconsider the purposes we have accepted
And to establish peace within ourselves.
The world presses on us too insistently;
The appetites too imperiously demand of us
And we forget to be real persons in ourselves.
May this moment be one of redemption,
Of renewal of faith in life and the living of it;
May the disciplines of humility and courage
Be strengthened from this time.
May it bring a rediscovery of self
And a lifting of the heart
With a sense of newness from that discovery—

New courage, fresh vigor, and a deeper
thoughtfulness
For the living of life from this day.

ROBERT T. WESTON
SEASONS OF THE SOUL, 1963

MORE THAN WE DESERVE

I heard the Second Brandenburg Concerto played
in honor of Bach's 300th birthday, and I was swept
away. I remembered a story about the people who
send messages into outer space. Someone suggested
sending a piece by Bach. The reply was: "But that
would be bragging."

Some say we get what we deserve in life, but I
don't believe it. We certainly don't deserve Bach.
What have I done to deserve the Second Brandenburg Concerto? I have not been kind enough; I
have not done enough justice; I have not loved my
neighbor, or myself, sufficiently; I have not praised
God enough to have earned a gift like this.

Life is a gift we have not earned and for which we
cannot pay. There is no necessity that there be a universe, no inevitability about a world moving toward
life and then self-consciousness. There might have
been . . . nothing at all.

Since we have not earned Bach—or crocuses or lovers—the best we can do is express our gratitude for the undeserved gifts, and do our share of the work of creation.

ROBERT R. WALSH
NOISY STONES, 1992

PICKING BLACKBERRIES

What will you give for a taste
of summer's last sweetness?
This jewelled crown of thorns
rings every path and highway;

No use pretending you
have not heard sweet temptation
chatter through the vines—
taste   eat

Put your hand in the thorns
and come out dripping juice,
king's purple spread from
hand to tongue.

Reach gently,
or you will find your thumb
full of thorns, and your pail
filled with unbearable tartness.

Reach gently, but reach.
The sweetest berries hide
toward the inside, hidden
beneath leaves barbed like critics.

Balance, if you must, precariously,
held by will and longing from
the net of thorns. If you want
the ripest fruit, relinquish safety.

Guard yourself only with these words:
Peril   abundance
whispered like a prayer
through purple lips.

LYNN UNGAR
BLESSING THE BREAD, 1996

THE TEACHING BEAN

When I was a child my stepmother gave me and my
sister each a lima bean. She showed us how to
dampen some blotting paper and line a jam jar with
it, and how to place the bean carefully between the
blotting paper and the jar. She told us to stand the
jars on the windowsill in our bedroom and keep the
blotting paper wet, and watch to see what would
happen.

A little later I took my bean out and polished it up with a bit of furniture polish. It was all shiny now and smelled much better than my sister's bean.

In a few days my sister's bean swelled and a strong white root pushed out of the bottom of the bean. My bean just sat there. A week later my sister's bean sprouted a green shoot that forced its way up and out of the top of the jar. My bean did nothing, but began to look wrinkly. In another week my sister's jar was full of roots and shoots and the bean was ready to be planted. My bean shriveled up and fell to the bottom of the jar and I threw it away.

How often have I covered things with furniture polish to make them shiny, to make them smell better? How often in my life have I cared more about the way things looked, and how they smelled, rather than how they really were? I spent half a lifetime covering my feelings with the emotional equivalent of furniture polish, thinking that if I looked good and smelled good the ache inside would go away.

But spirits are not like beans, thank god. They may shrivel with neglect, but as long as life persists there is the chance to wash off the polish and redeem the growing thing inside.

ELIZABETH TARBOX
EVENING TIDE, 1998

MORNING

Oh, it's nice to get up in the mornin',
But it's nicer to lie in bed.
SIR HARRY LAUDER

From the east comes the sun, bringing a new and
unspoiled day.

It has already circled the earth and look upon
distant lands and far-away peoples.

It has passed over mountain ranges and the waters
of the seven seas.
It has shone upon laborers in the fields, into the
windows of homes, and shops, and factories.

It has beheld proud cities with gleaming towers,
and also the hovels of the poor.

It has been witness to both good and evil, the works
of honest people, and the conspiracy of knaves.

It has seen marching armies, bomb-blasted villages
and "the destruction that wasteth at noonday."

Now, unsullied from its tireless journey, it comes to
us, messenger of the morning, harbinger of a new
day of light, and life, and hope.

Let not the dross of yesterday or the golden dreams
  of tomorrow dim the luster of this silver morn.

CLINTON LEE SCOTT
PROMISE OF SPRING, 1977

SONG

Say that air remembers lark
Say that sea remembers shark
Say that earth remembers mole
Say that fire remembers coal
  Who knows? Who knows?
  Time goes its way
  Whatever we say—

Say that hand remembers right
Say that eye remembers light
Say that mind remembers truth
Say that love remembers youth
  Who knows? Who knows?
  Time steals away
  Whatever we say—

CARL SEABURG
TO MEET THE ASKING YEARS, 1983

SHAKY SKATERS

Roller World is a typical roller rink that rents foul-smelling skates with fragile laces, and then pounds your ears senseless with hard-driving rock music. Roller World caters to people with no standards, no taste, and no class.

Like my family and myself.

I love Roller World. No one was born to skate, but there we all are, a roomful of unlikely skaters, doing our best. A few of course are hot shots, whizzing around on one foot, backwards half the time, breezy as you please. And another bunch, sad to say, is hopeless—their eight little wheels completely ignoring mission control. But round and round the rest of us go, steady and solid, one foot and then the next, in careful time to the Beastie Boys or Twisted Sister.

Folks look pretty darn good out there. I suppose I do too. No one knows that if even one word is spoken in my direction, I will lose my concentration and hit the floor hard. No one realizes that if they come up behind me too fast I will panic and crumble into the wall. No one can see that this steady skater is so precarious that the act of skating, just skating, takes everything.

As we roll around the rink, uncertain of our stride and rhythm, may we yet see the instability of

those who surround us. May we help when we are
steady, holding those who falter; may we calm the
reckless and urge the timid forward; may we keep
gentle company with the skaters at our side. Let us
move with the spirit of love, and may some quiet
presence help us with our laces at the end.

JANE RANNEY RZEPKA
A SMALL HEAVEN, 1989

WAITRESSING IN THE
SACRED KITCHENS

I love for a waitress to call me "Hon." It's comfort-
ing. She doesn't know me and I don't know her, but
we fit into well worn, ancient categories: I am the
Hungry One and she is the One Who Brings
Nourishment From the Unseen Source.

When I was younger, I worked as a waitress in
Philadelphia and New Jersey. I learned useful things
while serving food to strangers. I know how to rush
around with my hands full, thinking about six things
at the same time, which has stood me in good stead
as the working mother of two small sons. I know that
people are not at their best when they're hungry.
That knowledge helps me to understand world

events. If the citizens of the world were well fed, we'd have fewer wars and less mayhem.

The most helpful thing I grasped while waitressing was that some tables are my responsibility and some are not. A waitress gets overwhelmed if she has too many tables, and no one gets good service. In my life, I have certain things to take care of: my children, my relationships, my work, myself, and one or two causes. That's it. Other things are not my table. I would go nuts if I tried to take care of everyone, if I tried to make everybody do the right thing. If I went through my life without ever learning to say, "Sorry, that's not my table, Hon," I would burn out and be no good to anybody. I need to have a surly waitress inside myself that I can call on when it seems everyone in the world is waving an empty coffee cup in my direction. My Inner Waitress looks over at them, keeping her six plates balanced and her feet moving, and says, "Sorry, Hon, not my table."

One of the hardest lessons for me is learning how to blend my individuality with my role. I'm still learning this as a minister and as a therapist. I need a certain spiritual strength and a lessening of ego before I can take on a role and let people relate to me in my function as a therapist or a minister rather than as a fascinating woman with a birthday, a favorite color, a song I can sing better than it is on the album, and cool stories of travels to foreign lands. It's not easy to lose myself that way and I'm still not good at it.

When I was in seminary, all of us were struggling with how to blend and balance our individuality within the role of minister. We found that most people have a strong idea of how a minister should look and talk and behave. I can join a new group of people, talking and laughing, being normal, and the moment they find out I'm a minister the laughter dies as they check back over the things they've said in front of me, trying to remember if they've sworn or sinned or said something politically incorrect. It's hard. It makes some of us want to lie about what we do. It makes some ministers want to moon the group. That would banish those burdensome expectations.

There are times, though, when people need help to draw strength and comfort from the Spirit. As a minister, I'm the one who is there at the hospital or the funeral home. I'm the one who is there in my office when the family comes hoping for peace and clarity.

It is my job to bring nourishment to hungry souls from the sacred kitchens where the Spirit cooks up healing and comfort. It doesn't really matter at that moment when my birthday is, or that purple is my favorite color. What matters is the function I perform when I stand in the broad stream of history and symbol, faith and mythology, and let something larger than myself work through me, through the role I'm filling. What matters is that I'm smelling the rich aromas of hope and joy rising from the dishes I hold in my arms, and I know what it means to the people who need it.

Come sit down, Hon. Are you hungry?

MEG BARNHOUSE
THE ROCK OF AGES AT THE TAJ MAHAL, 1999

THE UNEXPECTED STAIRWAY

My husband and I had been at a small hotel in Bergen for two days before we discovered the stairway.

We had known it was there, of course. We had seen the sign, if not the thing itself. But we used the elevator. Saved time, we thought, and the energy we needed for exploring that charming Norwegian town on misty October days.

After breakfast on the third day, when the elevator seemed slow in arriving, my husband decided to walk up. He was waiting at the elevator door when I—and the elevator—arrived on the fourth floor.

"Let me show you something," he said, and led me back down the stairs he had just come up.

I was dazzled. Instead of the sterile, institutional look of most hotel stairways, this one had the warm beauty of an art-lover's home. There were bright paintings on all the walls, and at each landing a rug in jeweled tones, a table with fresh flowers, an exquisite chair or two. When we reached the first floor, we walked up again, filled with energy, drinking in the beauty.

"We might have missed this," I said.

"Have to be careful about saving time and losing life," he said.

BARBARA ROHDE
IN THE SIMPLE MORNING LIGHT, 1994

BOUNDLESSNESS

Dedicated to a dear friend in her nineties

I lie here in my body bound.
And yet—

My mother's smile—eight decades gone—
is clear and warm.

How can this be?
She's dead (or so I'm told) these eighty years.
And yet—

My greatniece has three dimples in her cheeks:
She always hesitates before she speaks
I see her smile and see my great grandfather,
(Who died before my birth and left no tintype
    likeness on this earth).

I lie here in my body bound.
And yet—

I feel again the squish of cool spring mud
    between my childhood toes.
I smell again the spice and cleanliness
    beqeathed by a wild pink rose.
I feel again the texture (sun-hot, lichen-
    fringed) of grey stone wall.
I cringe at shock of ice-salt surf;
    I glow, I splash—
    the seagulls call.

I lie here.
I wonder if thoughts have *their* chromosomes?
A seedlet through the worlds and eons roams
    and brushes by my mind
    intangible to this I call my brain—
    and inklings of its kernelled truths remain.
(and will not be cast out by any mortal doubt)

One year
it's likely I shall not be here in body bound.
And yet—

>The galaxies will whirl in cosmic
>cadence plain.
>I know I'll still be part of that
>—without the pain.

For things of value do not fade and die and end, but
blend into the great continuum called God by
some—by others left unnamed, lest naming limit
and define the endless goals of love.

WILLI BARBOUR
TO MEET THE ASKING YEARS, 1983

SUMMER'S END

One day a little boy was playing in front of his
house, when it occurred to him that he had never
seen an adult playing with a red wagon like his. And
he burst into tears.

When his mother asked why he was crying, the
boy said he was afraid that when he grew up he
wouldn't be able to play with his red wagon anymore.

The mother assured the child that when he grew
up he could play with his red wagon if he wanted to.

may experience our relationship to the force that gives us life.

It's like singing in the bathtub.

BRUCE T. MARSHALL
TAKING PICTURES OF GOD, 1996

DOG DAYS

Everyone needs a spiritual guide: a minister, rabbi, priest, therapist, or wise friend. My wise friend is my dog. He has deep insights to impart. He makes friends easily and doesn't hold a grudge. He enjoys simple pleasures and takes each day as it comes. Like a true Zen master, he eats when he's hungry and sleeps when he's tired. He's not hung up about sex. Best of all, he befriends me with an unconditional love that humans would do well to imitate.

Of course my dog does have his failings. He's afraid of firecrackers and hides in the closet whenever we run the vacuum cleaner. But unlike me, he's not afraid of what other people think of him or anxious about his public image. He barks at the mail carrier and the newsboy, but, in contrast to some people, I know he never growls at the children or barks at his spouse.

So my dog is a sort of guru. When I become too serious and preoccupied, he reminds me to frolic and play. When I get too wrapped up in abstractions and ideas, he reminds me to exercise and care for my body. On his own canine level, he shows me that it might be possible to live without inner conflicts or neuroses: uncomplicated, genuine, and glad to be alive.

Mark Twain remarked long ago that human beings have a lot to learn from the Higher Animals. Just because they haven't invented static cling, ICBM's, or television evangelists doesn't mean they aren't spiritually evolved. Let other people have their mentors, masters, and enlightened teachers. I have a doggone mutt.

GARY A. KOWALSKI
GREEN MOUNTAIN SPRING AND OTHER
LEAPS OF FAITH, 1997

THE SHIRK ETHIC

O God of Work and Leisure
Teach me to shirk on occasion,
Not only that I may work more effectively
But also that I may enjoy life more abundantly.
Enable me to understand that the earth

Magically continues spinning on its axis
Even when I am not tending thy vineyards.
Permit me to breathe more easily
Knowing the destiny of the race
Rests not on my shoulders alone.
Deliver me from false prophets who urge me
To "repent and shirk no more."
I pray for thy grace on me,
Thy faithful shirker.

RICHARD S. GILBERT
IN THE HOLY QUIET OF THIS HOUR, 1995

PATIENCE AND SILENCE

How quiet it is when we have the patience to be silent.
How much we can learn in moments like these.
> We can learn to have patience with ourselves,
>> to better understand and like who and what
>> we are.
> We can learn to have patience with others,
>> to better listen to what they say and how they
>> feel.
> We can learn to have patience with life,
>> to better work with it, rather than against it.
How much do we need silence:
> Silence for truth so that we may learn wisdom,

Silence for wisdom so that we may love,
Silence for love so that we may be just,
Silence for justice so that we may live fully.
May we be more patient and more silent,
    so that we may proceed with courage and
    compassion.

CHARLES A. GAINES
73 VOICES, 1972

MORE HUMAN

THAN OTHERWISE

WE ARE ALL MORE HUMAN
THAN OTHERWISE

The human race is a vast rainbow,
white, black, red, yellow, and brown
    bursting into view.
    Yet for all,
    blood is red,
    the sky is blue,
    the earth brown,
    the night dark.

In size and shape we are a varied pattern of
    tall and short,
    slim and stout,
    elegant and plain.
    Yet for all there are
    fingers to touch,
    hearts to break,
    eyes to cry,
    ears to hear,
    mouths to speak.

In tongue we are a tower of babel,
a great jumble of voices grasping for words,
groping for ways to say love, peace, pity, and hope.

Faiths compete, claiming the one way;
saviors abound, pointing to salvation.
Not all can be right, not one.
We are united only by our urge to search.

Boundaries divide us, lines drawn to mark our diversity,
maps charted to separate the human race from itself.
Yet a mother's grief,
a father's love,
a child's happy cry, a musician's sound,
an artist's stroke,
batter the boundaries and shatter the walls.

Strength and weakness,
arrogance and humility,
confidence and fear
live together in each one,
reminding us that we share a common humanity.
We are all more human than otherwise.

RICHARD S. GILBERT
IN THE HOLY QUIET OF THIS HOUR, 1995

REFLECTION

What is essential is never to allow
The limitations of time and the
Erosion of memories to deaden
The longing of the heart in
Its morning demand for love.

PAUL N. CARNES
LONGING OF THE HEART, 1973

IF LOVE BE THERE

This day,
Setting aside all that divides me from others;
This day,
Remembering that the world is beautiful
To him who is willing that it be so
And that into the open, eager heart
The beauty enters in
If love be there;
This day
I will make a part of the song of life.
There may be grief but if there be love it will be
    overcome.
There may be pain but it can be borne with dignity
    and courage;

There may be difficulty but it can be turned to
    strength.
Remembering that the world is beautiful
If I will let it be so for others whom I meet,
This day
I will make a part of the song of life.

ROBERT T. WESTON
SEASONS OF THE SOUL, 1963

WORDS

Let's keep talking, my love. Words we have to spare:
love words and angry words, and beneath them hurting, bleeding, dying words, and beneath them words
melted by fire and hardened by ice, words of sadness
and truth birthed from the cavern of tears.

And when the words are spent, heaped over the
pages and spilled to the floor, let us read each other's
eyes and see the chapters and the places where old
bookmarks press the pages apart, so the book opens
up to the old story before we can move on.

For you are all the love words I have ever heard
and all the hurt words where the love is deepest,
stripped back and bleeding.

But let's keep caring, ever so slowly building down
the words, one beneath the other, getting closer to

the truth and still deeper until I you touch your
words to my wounds, honor them, and feel the pain.
Our wounds may not be healed by the touch of the
other's words but are dignified by our recognition of
their existence.

Then and only then will the words mean anything; when we have used them up until the old
meanings have been scrubbed off; when the wrong
words have been tried and discarded and the right
words have been spoken in a whisper, then let us climb
down into each other's soul and rest there in the
silence, and love.

ELIZABETH TARBOX
LIFE TIDES, 1993

A LITANY OF RESTORATION

If, recognizing the interdependence of all life,
we strive to build community,
the strength we gather will be our salvation.

If you are black and I am white,
    IT WILL NOT MATTER.

If you are female and I am male,
    IT WILL NOT MATTER.

If you are older and I am younger,
   IT WILL NOT MATTER.

If you are liberal and I am conservative,
   IT WILL NOT MATTER.

If you are straight and I am gay,
   IT WILL NOT MATTER.

If you are Christian and I am Jewish,
   IT WILL NOT MATTER.

If we join spirits as brothers and sisters,
the pain of our aloneness will be lessened . . .
and that does matter.

   IN THIS SPIRIT, WE BUILD COMMUNITY
   AND MOVE TOWARD RESTORATION.

MARJORIE BOWENS-WHEATLEY
BEEN IN THE STORM SO LONG, 1991

A FRIENDLY ICE-CREAM BABY

It was a long journey on a cold winter day. Our
destination was Framingham, Massachusetts. Even
our wedding, nine years before, had been easier on
our nerves!

The shopping mall was one of those brick and plastic affairs with a slick New England facade and two banks for every store. I think it was designed by Mel Brooks.

We parked the car somewhere on the twenty acres of cement and walked to the Friendly Ice-Cream Store. Inside, we were pushed to a booth in the rear.

A listless waitress tried to memorize our order. Two hot fudge sundaes arrived as two chocolate sundaes. She appeared to be high on vanilla extract.

The store was crowded at noon. People were munching hamburgers, slurping coffee, and drowning in ice cream. They were for too busy to witness a miracle!

When the social worker arrived, she held a large screaming bundle in her arms. The customers muttered and groaned. "Get the baby out!" they seemed to say.

Little did they know I had just heard my daughter.

Little did they know I had just adopted a child.

Little did they know I had just seen the face of God.

I wonder: did the cries of the child in Bethlehem disturb the revelers at the inn?

DAVID O. RANKIN
PORTRAITS FROM THE CROSS, 1978

SUFFICIENCY

There is a limit to how much awe I can feel, even when I'm standing on a beach at dawn with all that religion means to me rolled out before my wondering eyes.

There is a limit to my acquisitiveness: I have more than enough stuff now. I have all the things I could possibly want to make my life comfortable. I have plenty of belongings, thank you.

But love, O God, there is no limit to my longing for love. Love is so elusive and so precious and doesn't follow any rules. I can't make people love me, or keep their love once I have it, or invest it in the bond market and draw on the interest. I can't catch love in a bottle and look at it in the afternoon when I'm lonely. I can't get love on demand with a bank card.

Knowing that love is not a limited resource, not an endangered species, doesn't help at all. What does it matter if there is a vast ocean of love out there, if I'm not able to immerse myself in it; if I'm locked up in here, without a drop of that ocean's moisture to bless me?

Here's what I can do. I can be open to the possibility of love. I can recognize love when it's offered. I can be vulnerable, knowing that those who dare not risk giving are unable to receive. I can admit

that being loved is an exercise in letting go, in sur-
rendering control, in being humbly grateful for
what is given.

I can accept love and let even the smallest
amount of it grow in me and shine out of me. I can
say at last: "The love that you give me is very good,
and it is enough."

ELIZABETH TARBOX
LIFE TIDES, 1993

SOME WISHES FOR YOU

I wish for you a troubled heart at times
As woes of world and friend come close beside
And keep you sleepless.
I wish for you the thrill of knowing
Who you are,
Where you stand,
And why.
Especially why.
Not prosperity, but dreams I wish for you;
Not riches, but a sense of your own worth I wish
For you.
Not even long life, however proud we'd be to
    have it so.
But life that is crammed with living,

Hour by hour.
And love I wish for you;
May you give it frequently.
I wish for you solitude in the midst of company,
And a mind full of company within your quiet
    times.
Full todays I wish for you, and full tomorrows.

CHARLES S. STEPHEN, JR.
THE GIFT OF THE ORDINARY, 1985

FOR MY FRIENDS WHO
ARE WOUNDED

If I could, I would go to them
And say, "It was only a dream."
I would sit beside them, and hold
Them in their dark, and let their tears
Fall on the soft sleeves of my gown.
I would kiss their hair. I would talk
Softly to them. I would tell them
The secrets of fireflies and stars
And the frost-lace on the windows
And the harvesting of corn.

I would sing the grandfather's songs.
I would bring small gifts in my hand:
White spiraled shells and crimson leaves,

Smooth stones, a hyacinth, a peach.
Then we would stand by the window,
Our arms around each other's waists.
We would breathe in the cold night air.
We would make promises and wait
Silently. Still. Listening for
the bright, brave, astonishing light.

BARBARA ROHDE
IN THE SIMPLE MORNING LIGHT, 1994

THE BOY WAS YOUNG

The boy was young (your son, my son).
He held life,
gentle and fragile as a wren's spotted egg,
in play-black-lined hands.

He brought it to me.
His eyebrows asked: What?
How should this find,
this all-that-he-had
glistening in its bed of dark sweat
be used?
What does it mean
to hold your life with your fingers?

How should I tell him how to live?
How do you tell someone you love
    humanity is frail
    (as he is frail, as you are frail)
    and mistakes will be made
    and life is fitting parts that don't belong?

RUDOLPH W. NEMSER
MOMENTS OF A SPRINGTIME, 1967

CONTACT

I stretch forth my hand
    Knowing not what I shall touch . . .
        A tender spot,
        An open wound,
        Warmth,
        Pulsing life,
        Fragile blossoms,
        A rock,
        Ice.

I am tentative, trembling . . .
    Wishing to avoid hurt,
    Wanting to link my life with Life.
        Lonely, I desire companions
        Naked, I long for defenders.

Lost, I want to find . . .
    to be found.
Will I touch strangers
  Or enemies
  Or nothing?

My hand is withdrawn
  But still it touches
    My vulnerable skin, my furrowed brow,
    My empty pocket, my full heart.
    Do others reach, tremble, withdraw?
    Do they desire, long, seek?
    Are they lonely, fearful, lost?
    Will they grasp a tentative, trembling hand?

I stretch forth my hand
  Knowing not what I shall touch . . .
  But hoping . . .

GORDON B. McKEEMAN
TO MEET THE ASKING YEARS, 1984

THE BLESSINGS OF AGE

One hears so much about the calamities of growing
old that at sixty I began to make a list of the things
that I like about my advancing years. My younger
friends suggested that I was merely playing Pollyana.

My older friends gently pointed out that my list might grow shorter as my life grows longer. Still, I made my list.

At the head of my list was this remarkable discovery: I was beginning to find the foibles of my friends and relatives endearing.

I could understand how, after observing the real tragedies of life for two-thirds of a century, one would become more tolerant of minor irritations. In a world filled with the suffering of the hungry and the homeless and the victims of violence, the cap left off the toothpaste tube does not loom very large.

But my fondness for these foibles came as a surprise to me. I suppose I finally have come to understand that when one loves, one loves the whole person, a person defined by foibles as well as strengths. Of course, there is still the flash of irritation, but these days when we say, "Isn't that just like him," more often than not, we say it with affection, with the same pleasure of recognition as when the letter in the mailbox is addressed in familiar handwriting.

Perhaps every long marriage follows these five stages: 1. Darling, you are perfect. 2. Good grief! You seem to have a few foibles. 3. Let me help you get rid of your foibles so you will indeed be perfect. 4. Okay, I love you in spite of your foibles. 5. I can't believe this has happened. I sometimes love you because of your foibles.

I recently made the wonderful discovery that "foible" originally meant the weak part of a sword, from the center to the tip, while "forte" referred to the sword's stronger part. That says something to me about accepting our weaknesses while holding on to our strengths. Who would want to go out to meet a dragon with only half a sword?

BARBARA ROHDE
IN THE SIMPLE MORNING LIGHT, 1994

PRAYER FOR THOSE GATHERED IN WORSHIP

In this familiar place, listen:
to the sounds of breathing, creaking chairs,
shuffling feet, clearing throats, and sighing all around
Know that each breath, movement, the glance
meant for you or intercepted
holds a life within it.

These are signs
that we choose to be in this company
have things to say to each other
things not yet said but in each other's presence still
    trembling behind our hearts' doors
these doors closed but unlocked
each silent thing waiting

on the threshold between unknowing and knowing,
between being hidden and being known.

Find the silence among these people
and listen to it all—breathing, sighs,
movement, holding back—
hear the tears that have not yet reached their eyes
perhaps they are your own
hear also the laughter building deep where joy abides
despite everything.
Listen: rejoice. And say Amen.

BARBARA PESCAN
MORNING WATCH, 1999

OUGHT TO

I cannot love
because I ought to.
I cannot hope
because I ought to.
I cannot believe
because I ought to
or because I want to
or am taught to
or because
it is reasonable
or desirable

or possible
for someone else.
I can only love
and hope
and believe
sometimes or often,
not quite or almost,
seldom or never really
and I need you
in between.

J. DONALD JOHNSTON
BEGINNING NOW, 1970

FORGIVENESS

There is incredible power in forgiveness. But forgiveness is not rational. One can seldom find a reason to forgive or be forgiven. Forgiveness is often undeserved. It may require a dimension of justice (penance, in traditional terms), but not always, for what it holds sacred is not fairness, but self-respect and community. Forgiveness does not wipe away guilt, but invites reconciliation. And it is as important to be able to forgive as it is to be forgiven.

No, we do not forgive and forget. But when we invite the power of forgiveness, we release ourselves from some of the destructive hold the past has on us. Our hatred, our anger, our need to feel wronged—those will destroy us, whether a relationship is reconciled or not.

But we cannot just will ourselves to enter into forgiveness, either as givers or receivers. We can know it is right and that we want to do it and still not be able to.

We can, however, be open and receptive to the power of forgiveness, which, like any gift of the spirit, isn't of our own making. Its power is rooted in love. The Greek word for this kind of love is *agape*. Martin Luther King, Jr., defined *agape* as "Love seeking to preserve and create community." This kind of love is human, but it is also the grace of a transcendent power that lifts us out of ourselves. It transforms and heals; and even when we are separated by time or space or death, it reconciles us to ourselves and to Life. For its power abides not just between us but within us. If we invited the power of *agape* to heal our personal wounds and give us the gift of forgiveness, we would give our world a better chance of survival.

SARA MOORES CAMPBELL
INTO THE WILDERNESS, 1990

WHEN MY ANGER'S OVER

When my anger's over
may the world be young again
as after rain—
the cool clean promise
and the dance
of branches glistening green.

RAYMOND JOHN BAUGHAN
THE SOUND OF SILENCE, 1965

PRAYER IN ACTION

A number of years ago, my brother lay dying in the hospital. He spent days in the intensive care unit while members of my family, including my mother, sat for many long hours on chairs in the hallway outside his room. Among visitors who came to share the vigil was a member of our church.

"How are you doing?" the friend asked.

My mother was too exhausted to tell anything but the truth. "I'm tired," she said. "I'm very, very tired. I'm too tired to even pray any more."

"But don't you see," her friend replied, "your very presence here is a prayer."

There are times when all words fail us, all forms seem hollow, and no one out there or inside seems to be listening. At those times, our presence, just our presence, is prayer. Our bodies, our actions, become our prayer, our connection to God, whatever God may be.

JANE ELLEN MAULDIN
GLORY HALLELUJAH! NOW PLEASE PICK UP YOUR SOCKS, 1998

TRADITIONAL MARRIAGE

I'm a bit confused. In Spartanburg there are large billboards that say, "Our community supports traditional marriage." Well, yeah. I'm trying to think of ways to support traditional marriage. Then I get to thinking, what is a traditional marriage? Maybe I think too much. A traditional marriage? How far back are we going for these traditions? Because if we go back to biblical times, we have the traditional marriage of Abraham where he and his wife traveled quite a bit. A couple of times when Abraham was in fear of his life he lied and said his wife was his sister, so the Pharaoh took her for one of his concubines. Then when the Pharaoh found out, he threw them both out of the country for violating *his* traditional morals, which dictated you don't do things like that.

Or are we talking about the traditional marriage of Isaac where his father sent a servant to pick out a wife for him, and the servant brought her back to Isaac who took her into his tent and made her his wife? Or their son Jacob's marriage, where he worked seven years for Rachel and then was given her older sister in a sneaky way after he had drunk enough at the wedding feast not to know the difference until it was too late? Then he married Rachel, too.

Are we talking about traditional marriages where the parents decide who their children are going to marry? Are we talking about traditional American marriages? American marriages from the 1600s? The Victorian Era, where women were not allowed to have anesthesia during childbirth, not allowed to own property, not even legally considered to have custody of their children?

Just how far back into history are we supposed to go? Back to the last century when there was no birth control information to be had? When it was not illegal for a man to beat his wife or rape her? No wait, that wasn't the last century. In South Carolina, that was the early eighties. I'd be willing to talk about supporting traditional marriage if people would have the manners to tell me what it is they want me to support.

Someone told me that traditional marriage means marriage between a man and a woman, but I said that couldn't be it. Why would marriage between a man and a woman need any more support than it already has? It's the only kind of marriage that's legal. It's the kind of marriage almost everyone has. It's the kind you see on TV and the only kind little kids are taught about in school and the only kind that is mentioned in books and the only kind you see pictures of in magazines. How much more support than that do they want?

If marriage between a man and a woman is the one they want us to support, that would mean they were against samegendered people joining together in commitment. That can't be it. The Christian Right is *for* marriage, right? They support commitment between two people. It is what makes our society stable. Gay people being able to marry wouldn't threaten marriages between men and women. I mean, it's not as if legalizing same-sex marriage would suddenly make men all over the place say, "Oh, golly, I *was* going to marry a woman, but now I think I'll marry a man." Or women saying, "You know, I had been dreaming of marrying a man, but now that it's legal to marry my best friend, I think I'll do that!" On second thought, that last one

sounds pretty good. Marrying my best friend.
Hmmm. I must think about those billboards some
more.

MEG BARNHOUSE
THE ROCK OF AGES AT THE TAJ MAHAL, 1999

SPEECH STAMMERS TO TELL

Speech stammers to tell
of touch of stone, of love,
of ache inside,
or startle of surprise.

Whatever at last is said
is spoken from
what is unsayable.

RAYMOND JOHN BAUGHAN
THE SOUND OF SILENCE, 1965

FAULT LINE

FAULT LINE

Did you ever think there might be a fault line
passing underneath your living room:
a place in which your life is lived in meeting
and in separating, wondering
and telling, unaware that just beneath
you is the unseen seam of great plates
that strain through time? And that your life, already
spilling over the brim, could be invaded,
sent off in a new direction, turned
aside by forces you were warned about
but not prepared for? Shelves could be spilled out,
the level floor set at an angle in
some seconds' shaking. You would have to take
your losses, do whatever must be done
next.
    When the great plates slip
and the earth shivers and the flaw is seen
to lie in what you trusted most, look not
to more solidity, to weighty slabs
of concrete poured or strength of cantilevered
beam to save the fractured order. Trust
more the tensile strands of love that bend
and stretch to hold you in the web of life
that's often torn but always healing. There's
your strength. The shifting plates, the restive earth,

your room, your precious life, they all proceed
from love, the ground on which we walk together.

ROBERT R. WALSH
NOISY STONES, 1992

EN ROUTE TO DEATH

Autumn, we know,
Is life en route to death.
The asters are but harbingers of frost.
The trees, flaunting their colors at the sky,
In other times will follow where the leaves have fallen,
And so shall we.
Yet other lives will come: new Beethovens
And Miltons will arise,
Their genius nourished by the thoughts we leave
As we on Milton and on Beethoven
Our spirits fed.
So may we know, accept, embrace,
The mystery of life we hold a while
Nor mourn that it outgrows each separate self,
But still rejoice that we may have our day.
Lift high our colors to the sky! and give,
Each in his time, fresh glory to the earth.
Thus may we grow to know and cherish
That unity which in each moment warms our hearts,

Flowing from each to each,
Making us, part with part,
A wholeness we could never be alone.
Thus may we find a kinship with all life,
Reaching across all barriers of race,
Philosophies and creeds,
Making us one with everything that lives
And, as with our inmost atom, each bright star.

ROBERT T. WESTON
SEASONS OF THE SOUL, 1963

THE LEGACY OF CARING

Despair is my private pain
    Born from what I have failed to say
        failed to do
        failed to overcome.
Be still my inner self
        let me rise to you
        let me reach down into your pain
        and soothe you.
I turn to you
        to renew my life
I turn to the world
        the streets of the city
            the worn tapestries of

brokerage firms
crack dealers
private estates
personal things in the bag lady's cart
rage and pain in the faces that turn from me
afraid of their own inner worlds.
This common world I love anew
as the life blood of generations
who refused to surrender their humanity
in an inhumane world
courses through my veins.
From within this world
my despair is transformed to hope
and I begin anew
the legacy of caring.

THANDEKA
BEEN IN THE STORM SO LONG, 1991

THANKS TO THE FRIENDLY, FAMILIAR

I went to the beach, and rested there, intent on prayer. For my soul was heavy and I had to hear things I wanted God to hear.

But some flighty flock kept interrupting my thoughts. I don't know the make of bird but there were a lot of them, hanging off the bare branches of the birch trees, twittering with ferocious excitement. I knew they were getting ready to leave, and at once I wanted to be with them, flying in that geometric formation, right in the middle of the flock, able to look right and left and see only familiar shapes and hear friendly voices.

But I am too heavy. One of my thoughts weighed more than several of those birds together. So they flew in formation, cutting an arc across the face of the morning and were gone. And I was alone.

I closed my eyes and there was no discernible sound, except a hum of traffic perhaps a mile away. The ocean doesn't sing, the sky makes no sound, the earth doesn't creak in its daily round. Solitude is no symphony, and I felt that I belonged not to the sand nor the sea nor the sky, but only to the quiet.

Then, I was shaken by a familiar discordant voice: a gull flying overhead, hanging in space, who wasn't going anywhere. The voice of the gull was the sweetest note I had ever heard.

Thank God for the gulls who are not afraid of the storm, who do not leave when winter comes.

ELIZABETH TARBOX
EVENING TIDE, 1998

AUTUMN SPEAKS

Out of doors
The colors of bright autumn and the bright sun
Tell of the beauty of that which dies
But always comes again.
They speak directly to the heart
Of the eternal which outlives all moments
And yet lives only in them,
Outlives all forms, yet comes again in them as in
    ourselves.
It is said that there is nothing new in the world,
No thoughts, even, which others have not thought
Yet every thought is new to him who for himself
Thinks it for the first time.
Each miracle of life is also rebirth, life born again,
Though every individual be new,
Existing at his birth for his first time.
Life in each one, as in the leaf and flower,
Accepts and yet cheats death.
There is a sadness in the autumn leaf: I feel a sorrow
    that its beauty dies
And feel its message for the lives of those,
As of myself, whom I have known and loved.
The leaf comes not again, though other leaves
And flowers will bloom, and other lives,
Richer that we have been, shall take our place.

Perhaps the autumn teaches us a wiser grace
Through which we live, by learning to let go.

ROBERT T. WESTON
SEASONS OF THE SOUL, 1963

ESSENTIAL WISDOM

Living brings you death; there is no other road.
GALWAY KINNELL

All flesh is grass.
ISAIAH 40:6

E. B. White once wrote of his difficult dog, Fred:
"Life without him would be heaven, but I'm afraid it
is not what I want."

That seems to me to be a piece of essential wisdom that should never be lost. It is broad, as essential wisdom ought to be, and touches more than E.
B. White's mangy dog, Fred.

Life without a lot of the Freds of our lives would
be heaven, or so at least it appears at first light. A
lingering Nebraska winter is a kind of Fred, but life
without winter is not really what I want. Life without
conflict or unhappiness has certain appeals, but ever
since we were expelled from Eden it has been thus,

and who can imagine a worthwhile life without them?

Life without the pain of loss would be heaven, but I'm afraid it is not what any of us would take. I think we really don't want heaven. What we want is full and worthwhile life, outlined as it is by its limitations. What we want is not life without sorrow, but a full-ness of experience that absorbs sorrow and joy, Nebraska winters and springs, living and dying.

CHARLES S. STEPHENS, JR.
THE GIFT OF THE ORDINARY, 1985

LEGACY

Maybe love does not die, is not obliterated by hurts or anger. Maybe love does not dissipate, or sink like silt to dry out in the sun. Maybe love is not wasted or silly, or found to be something other than love.

Perhaps the love that settled about our shoulders and caressed us for a spell was created by ancient lovers from Sumer and Pompeii, blown by the winds around the South China sea, gathering strength across continents and through centuries. When we let go of it, perhaps it floated on, embracing other strangers unexpectedly, who turn toward each other, seeing the other for the first time, changed by the cloud of love that has gathered them together. Oh, my dear, do not despair that love has come and gone. Although we are broken, the love that spilled out of us has joined the love that circles the world and makes it blessed.

ELIZABETH TARBOX
EVENING TIDE, 1998

THE IDIOCY OF FLIGHT

A well-known poem by Robert Graves speaks of butterflies—their "honest idiocy of flight," "lurching here and there by guess and God and hope and hopelessness." Any number of quotations sound this way, and so, I think do we. But privately.

Publicly we speak the civilized language of human beings who have things under control. No idiocy, no lurching. The world sees that we function well and happily. Other people believe it, and even we begin to believe it. Life moves forward as always.

Privately, though, we experience long stretches of turbulence and the occasional sudden downdraft. So many in our church feel alone when things go poorly at home, when they feel their age (whatever it is), or when they grieve. So many feel alone in their money worries or career problems. Awful life situations seem to set us apart from one another.

Normal lives include these awful parts. They don't always show from the outside; it's hard to believe any other folks at coffee hour are feeling the same kinds of screaming pain, or emptiness, or entrapment, or panic, or precariousness, or low-grade worry. Lives, even lives well-lived, don't stay in place for long—at least that's how it seems from the peculiar vantage point of the minister's study.

It's a help, I think, to accept "the idiocy of flight," the butterfly flight-pattern so firmly implanted in the human mind and heart. Let the lurching, then, be no surprise, and know we're all up there flying every which way, together.

JANE RANNEY RZEPKA
A SMALL HEAVEN, 1989

HEAVEN IN A WILDFLOWER

She stared out the window and smiled.

Miss Sweeney was almost gone. A wisp of white hair, two brown eyes, small thin lips, and a quivering body were all that remained.

She stared out the window and smiled.

After 48 years of teaching—and 87 years of life—
and six years paralyzed from the neck down—Miss
Sweeney seemed to be part of another world.

She stared out the window and smiled.

Miss Sweeney was tied to the bed. She could no
longer speak an intelligible word, or move her head
from side to side, or even chew her food.

She stared out the window and smiled.

After she died, I returned to her room to collect
her belongings. From the bed I could see the
expanse of sky and the single limb of a tree. A robin
was nesting in Miss Sweeney's world.

I stared out the window and smiled.

DAVID O. RANKIN
PORTRAITS FROM THE CROSS, 1978

COMFORT YE MY PEOPLE

I wasn't flattered when one of my daughters confided
that she had thought of me as "The Big There-
There" when she was three years old. If I remember
correctly, I was in the middle of a phase where I was
hoping to reassure myself that I still had a fertile
mind as well as a welcoming bosom.

Now, years later, I can admit that the role of Big
There-There is a necessary part of parenthood not

to be disparaged. At times even the most mature of us want someone to dry our eyes, encircle us with welcoming arms, and offer us a cup of hot cocoa. I shall be forever grateful to my friend Ruth, who interrupted her political campaign to ride to the hospital, make her way past the folks in intensive care with convincing stories that I was her little sister, and reach bravely through the thicket of I.V.s, heart monitors, and breathing tubes to embrace me.

Still, the origin of the word "comfort" means, "to make strong." As comforters, we often believe we have to take away the pain, only to discover that we are only able to help those in pain find the sources of their own strength. At times it is our mere presence. "I am here. I see your suffering. I care for you." At times it is a helping hand. "I'll vacuum. I'll wash up these dishes. I'll drive you." At times, it is a few words that put things in perspective.

We're never quite sure what will truly comfort another, or what special act will comfort us. We go looking for a "Big There-There" and find instead that the excitement of a new idea lifts us from despair. I expected little solace from my frail ninety-year-old father when he called me in the hospital to see how I was, but when he called me "Punky" for the first time in fifty-four years, I felt the fidelity of that relationship. My narrow room was filled with memory and hope.

Perhaps those of us who would be comforters
could learn from the medieval scholastic who wrote
so long ago, "Work, therefore, in what you do, from
love and not from fear."

If we can put aside our fear that we might say or
do something to add inadvertently to the suffering
of those we would comfort, if we can put aside our
fear of our own loss or the pain of our own pity,
then love might find its way of bringing strength to
the weak and light to those in the shadows.

BARBARA ROHDE
IN THE SIMPLE MORNING LIGHT, 1994

SHE SPEAKS OF DEATH

For J. V.

Oblivion, she said
in a weary voice,
is what is after death.
    There is nothing after death
    but nothing
    and that's all right with me.

It made good scientific sense,
nailed to the cathedral door
of her religious childhood.

And when her husband died
a few years later
oblivion
pinned against eternity
sagged in the middle
and in its folds
sweet disbelief surprised her
and the hope
she hadn't seen the last of him yet.

BARBARA PESCAN
MORNING WATCH, 1999

A TIME TO CRY

The mother waited for her child at the bus stop. The
bus arrived on time, depositing the passengers on
the other side of the highway.

The eight-year-old boy broke from the group and
began running across the four lanes of concrete.
The blue Cadillac crushed him like a plastic doll.

In the living-room that day:

> You tell her to speak to God.
> You tell her to eat and to sleep.
> You tell her to look to the future.
> You tell her to walk in the cool air.

You tell her to bear the pain and sorrow.

You tell her to think of the other children.

But your face is wet with tears; and your heart is gripped by grief; and your mind is lost in darkness; and your soul plunges wildly into the desolation of the valley—where all words are symbols of absurdity.

Yes, there will be another day. But today—there is nothing to do but share the tragedy. There is nothing to do but cry!

DAVID O. RANKIN
PORTRAITS FROM THE CROSS, 1978

THE COST

Death is not too high a price to pay
for having lived. Mountains never die,
nor do the seas or rocks or endless sky.
Through countless centuries of time, they stay
eternal, deathless. Yet they never live!
If choice there were, I would not hesitate
to choose mortality. Whatever Fate
demanded in return for life I'd give,
for, never to have seen the fertile plains
nor heard the winds nor felt the warm sun on sands
beside the salty sea, nor touched the hands
of those I love—without these, all the gains

of timelessness would not be worth one day
of living and of loving; come what may.

DOROTHY N. MONROE
STOPPING PLACES, 1974

LET ME DIE LAUGHING

We are all dying, our lives always moving toward
completion.

We need to learn to live with death, and to
understand that death is not the worst of all events.

We need to fear not death, but life—

    empty lives,

    loveless lives,

    lives that do not build upon the gifts that each of
        us have been given,

    lives that are like living deaths,

    lives which we never take the time to savor and
        appreciate,

    lives in which we never pause to breathe deeply.

What we need to fear is not death, but squander-
ing the lives we have been miraculously given.

So let me die laughing, savoring one of life's crazy
moments. Let me die holding the hand of one I love,
and recalling that I tried to love and was loved in
return. Let me die remembering that life has been

good, and that I did what I could. But today, just
remind me that I am dying so that I can live, savor,
and love with all my heart.

MARK MORRISON-REED
BEEN IN THE STORM SO LONG, 1991

BECAUSE WE MEAN IT

May those who follow after us sense our happiness,
our involvement, our feeling of self-worth and group
accomplishment. May we share with them not only
our fears and uncertainties, but also the style with
which we face-down our troubles and shortcomings.
Whether in laughing bravado or in steadfast deter-
mination, may we leave examples of endurance, of
wisdom, of joy, and of compassion. From our persist-
ent stance, may those who follow learn of bravery
and generous living.

Life has a sweetness and a charm, for all its manifold failures and shortcomings and torments. A few
years of peace, a few crusts of bread, a few words of
love—and even the most pessimistic want to run the
risks of life. It takes so little to make us happy, and
so much to make us sad. If this were not so, the
human race long since would have given up! We are
here because we have not given up. We are here to

continue to risk all for life. We are here because we
mean it!

ROBERT MARSHALL
73 VOICES, 1972

WHEN LIFE IS MESSY

It is easy to pray when the sun shines
And we are grateful for another glorious day of being.
It is hard to pray when wind and rain and thunder
Plague our every step and spoil our every plan.

It is easy to be virtuous when life goes well
And our existence is a journey from bliss to beauty
    and back.
It is hard to be virtuous when life assaults us
And our very being is a pilgrimage from bad to
    worse to worst.

It is easy to be cheerful when health bursts in us
So that we can feel the very pulse of life.
It is hard to be happy when pain and fatigue beset us
And we wonder if we can go on.

It is easy to do good when our goodness is rewarded
And we feel the power of pride in accomplishment.

It is hard to do good when we suffer for our efforts
And are troubled because we have been
    misunderstood.

It is easy to feel religious impulses well up inside us
When inspiration lives at our elbow and walks on
    our path.
It is hard to feel religious when we are tired with
    work to be done
And discouragement seems to mark our every move.

O God of order and neatness, we give thanks for all
    that is good.
We are grateful for manifold blessings bestowed
    upon us.
O God of chaos and disorder, be with us also when
    life is messy.
Bless our coming in and our going out from this day
    forth.

RICHARD S. GILBERT
IN THE HOLY QUIET OF THIS HOUR, 1995

IT TOUCHES US

I SAY IT TOUCHES US

I say that it touches us that our blood is
    sea water and our tears are salt, that the
    seed of our bodies is scarcely different
    from the same cells in a seaweed,
    and that the stuff of our bones is like the coral.

I say that the tide rolls in on us, whether
    we like it or no, and the sands of time
    keep running their intended course.

I say we have to go down into the wave's trough
    to find ourselves, and then ride her swell
    until we can see beyond ourselves into
    our neighbors eye.

I say that we shall never leave the harbor
    if we do not hoist the sail.

I say that we have got to walk the waves
    as well as solid ground.

I say that anyone who goes without
    consciousness of this will remain
    chained to a rusty anchor.

May the journey find us worthy. Amen.

MARNI P. HARMONY
EXALTATION, 1987

THE WEB OF LIFE

There is a living web that runs through us
To all the universe
Linking us each with each and through all life
On to the distant stars.
Each knows a little corner of the world, and lives
As if this were his all.
We no more see the farther reaches of the threads
Than we see of the future, yet they're there.
Touch but one thread, no matter which;
The thoughtful eye may trace to distant lands
Its firm continuing strand, yet lose its filaments as
    they reach out,
But find at last it coming back to him from whom it
    led.
We move as in a fog, aware of self
But only dimly conscious of the rest
As they are close to us in sight or feeling.
New objects loom up for a time, fade in and out;
Then, sometimes, as we look on unawares, the fog
    lifts
And there's the web in shimmering beauty,
Reaching past all horizons. We catch our breath;
Stretch out our eager hands, and then
In comes the fog again, and we go on,
Feeling a little foolish, doubting what we had seen.

The hands were right. The web is real.
Our folly is that we so soon forget.

ROBERT T. WESTON
SEASONS OF THE SOUL, 1963

YOU BE GLAD AT THAT STAR

Several years ago and shortly after twilight our 3½-year-old tried to gain his parents' attention to a shining star.

The parents were busy with time and schedules, the irritabilities of the day and other worthy preoccupations. "Yes, yes, we see the star—now I'm busy, don't bother me." On hearing this the young one launched through the porch door, fixed us with a fiery gaze and said, "You be glad at that star!"

I will not forget the incident or his perfect words. It was one of those rare moments when you get everything you need for the good of your soul—reprimand, disclosure and blessing. It was especially good for me, that surprising moment, because I am one who responds automatically and negatively to the usual exhortations to pause-and-be-more-appreciative-of-life-unquote. Fortunately, I was caught grandly off guard.

There is a notion, with some truth in it, that we cannot command joy, happiness, appreciation, fulfillment. We do not engineer the seasons of the soul or enjoin the quality of mood in another, and yet, I do believe there is right and wisdom in that imperative declaration—you be glad at that star!

If we cannot impel ourselves into a stellar gladness, we can at least clean the dust from the lens of our perception; if we cannot dictate our own fulfillment, we can at least steer in the right direction; if we cannot exact a guarantee for a more appreciative awareness of our world—for persons and stars and breathing and tastes and the incalculable gift of every day—we can at least prescribe some of the conditions through which an increased awareness is more likely to open up the skies, for us and for our children.

It is not always the great evils that obstruct and waylay our joy. It is our unnecessary and undignified surrender to the petty enemies: and I suggest it is our duty to scheme against them and make them subservient to human decree—time and schedules, our irritabilities of the day, and other worthy preoccupations. Matters more subtle and humane should command our lives. You be glad at that star.

Fret not yourself, it tends only to evil.
PSALM 37:8

CLARKE WELLS
THE STRANGENESS OF THIS BUSINESS, 1975

A BAPTISM

She called to ask if I would baptize her infant son.

I said, "What we do is like a baptism, but not exactly. And we normally do it only for people who are part of the church family. The next one we have scheduled is in May."

She said, "Could we come to talk with you about it anyway?"

They came to see me, the very young woman and her child and the child's very young father.

She explained that the child had been born with a heart defect. He had to have a risky heart operation soon. She had asked the clergyman of her own church if he would baptize her son, and he had refused because she was not married to the baby's father.

I told them that their not being married would not be an impediment to anything we might do, but that our child dedication ceremony still might not be what they were looking for.

I explained that our ceremony does not wash away any sin, it does not guarantee the child a place in heaven, it doesn't even make the child a member of the church.

In fact, I said, it doesn't change the child at all. What we expect is that it will change the rest of us in our relationship with the child, and with all children.

She listened patiently.

When I was through she said, "All I want is to know that God blesses my baby."

In my mind I gasped at the sudden clarity in the room.

I said, with a catch in my throat, "I think I can do that."

And I did.

ROBERT R. WALSH
NOISY STONES, 1992

O MYSTERY!

O mystery beyond my understanding,
Voice in my heart answering to the earth,
And light of distant stars!
O wonder of the spring, leading the seasons on:
The dewdrops sparkling on the web at sunrise,
And unseen life, moving in depths and shallows of
    the brook,
Trembling in raindrops at the edge of eaves,
Whisper to me of secrets I would know.

O Power that flows through me and all that is,
Light of stars, pulsating in the atoms in my heart,
Whether you are mind and spirit
Or energy transcending human thought
I cannot know, and yet I feel
That out of pain and sorrow and the toil
Through which creation springs from human hands
A force works toward the victory of life, even
    through the stars.
Here on the earth winter yields slowly, strikes again,
    and hard,
And lovely buds, advance guards of the spring, suffer
    harsh death,
And pity moves the heart.
Yet life keeps pulsing on.
The stars still shine, the sun rises again,
New buds burst forth, and life still presses on.
O mystery!
I lift my eyes in wonder and in awe!

ROBERT T. WESTON
SEASONS OF THE SOUL, 1963

PREFACE

I thought I heard the voice of the spirit cry:

Come and find me. You won't have to look hard.
Come to where the ocean touches the shore; find
me in the bright-light promise of morning on the
waves; look carefully at the bubbles breaking on the
wet sand—there I am. Turn over the glistening rock,
slippery with its cushion of seaweed—here I am.
Hear the gulls crying news of the endless ocean—
that is my news, my voice. Lie with me in the tall,
green marsh grass; see my footprints in the sand you
have walked upon. Do not say I am lost, for you have
found me. I am here.

ELIZABETH TARBOX
LIFE TIDES, 1993

PRAYER

if there is a god
i think he must be shaped something like a mountain
and something like a tree
and something like an ocean . . .

i rather imagine he looks something like a black man
and something like a white man
and something like a yellow man
and something like a woman, too . . .
i think he sees the universe through the eyes
of a big, brown bear
and through the eyes of a dove
and through the eyes of a gentle, medium-size whale . . .
i rather suspect that he happened
something like a small child's smile happens,
mysteriously,
but as unavoidable as the morning,
and i think he treasures his friendship with the stars
the way another star does . . .
and, finally,
i imagine he is as much afraid of death,
of nothingness,
as i am,
and that there are moments
when he wonders if he is real . . . .

J. DAVID SCHEYER
73 VOICES, 1972

EMERGENT LIFE

I am amazed, and all but mute with awe
That on this cinder, hurtling around the sun,
A living thing arose, to clothe the earth;
That all this splendor of the leaf and flower,
Life in the sea and on the earth,
From crawling thing to singing bird and man,
All fruit of the same life, continually renewed
Through cell and seed and birth—
In spite of winter's storms that sweep the earth,
This miracle of shared and sharing life,
Arose and, still evolving, still goes on.
Here on this whirling ball warmed by the sun
(As on what planets of what other stars?)
Through countless deaths and many million forms
Life bore its varied cells,
And there were those from which the coral grew
To atolls in the sea;
The fish, the insects and the nesting birds
All played their varied parts through which
A widening community spread across the earth.
Thus as through us the same life flows through all
Making us debtor and creditor, brother and sister,
    each of all;
Each as the grass, springing from common earth,
Adding to others and receiving as well,
And all of us, seed, plant and flower and seed

En route through love and the awakening mind
To what we cannot guess.

ROBERT T. WESTON
SEASONS OF THE SOUL, 1963

A TRILOBITE POET

Two birds call back and forth, echoing a secret not
shared with me . . .

It's one of those moments when my senses are
seduced. The ocean flows through my fingers, and I
am flooded with the love songs of seabirds; I am the
color of sand and the texture of marsh grass.

I tinker with metaphor and alliteration, I fool
with mirages and moods. I am a word person.
There's a poet buried in me—fossil hard and silent
as stone—a trilobite poet who leans out to you, longing to touch your poet and be understood; no clever
words, just a leaning out, and a touching and an
understanding.

All the poets who have leaned out and taught me
what love is are pressed into that fossil poet in me;
all the endless eras of waiting and the stomachache
fear of disappointment are compressed there.
Petrified dreams lie frozen, buried beneath layers of
words. It's all there, hardened within the age-old

shell of my Paleozoic self, waiting to be exhumed by
the call of wild birds fishing the dark ocean, waiting
to be touched and warmed by the silent poet in you.

ELIZABETH TARBOX
LIFE TIDES, 1993

FOR HUMILITY

Holy Spirit, whose name is Timeless, and who hast
appeared to those who seek Thee in many forms
and images, we would seek Thee as Thou art. But if
by reason of our humanity thy true self be hidden
from our eyes, let this not be the cause of our weary-
ing of our quest, or of our mistaking an appearance
for reality, and thereby failing into sin by assuming
that by our knowledge we have become Thine own
chosen people.

 O God, we are a peculiar people—often doubting
where others so easily trust; rejecting that salvation
offered through sacrament and creed, bell, book
and candle, to seek we know not what; tentative and
often contentious. Only save us from the false belief
that any virtue lies in our peculiarity, and may our
uncertainty not arise from indifference or fear of

commitment, but from a longing for and a love of the Truth.

PAUL N. CARNES
LONGING OF THE HEART, 1973

THE RESTLESSNESS OF THOUGHT

For a little while I would like to escape
The nagging reminders of my body and the world.
I would like every restlessness to be stilled,
    except that of thought,
And let my eager mind race out
To reach beyond all bounds of time and space
Or turn, and look within, to the inmost core of
    being.
I would like to be freed from the demands
Of necessity, ambition and desire, to commune
    with myself
And to leap across the abyss of the unknown
To listen for the voice of the universe
As it might speak through me.
I would feel myself one with the stars and know
    their patience
As they swing through space,
Where perhaps forms of life and mind

Blossom on planets whirling around them
Beyond any forms and qualities our minds could
    grasp.
I would seek in this moment to catch a glimpse
Of meanings that might include all of this with us,
Have awareness of beauty beginning
Where the human mind leaves off,
This day and this moment knowing myself
One with all being.
I would be silent and let infinity speak through me
To create in myself a greater patience
And passion
For our still unknown and undetermined ends.

ROBERT T. WESTON
SEASONS OF THE SOUL, 1963

SILENCE

You cannot judge the importance of things
by the noise they make.
JAMES HILTON
GOOD-BYE MR. CHIPS

The stars in their courses make no noise.

We do not hear the grinding of gears
    with the turning of the earth.

The reliable forces of nature are quiet forces.
  Dawn arrives with no blare of trumpets,
  and night needs no bugle blast to announce its
    approach.

Silent forces work upon soil and seed.
  The growing corn inaudibly unfolds.

Power is not in the loudness of the thunder,
  but in the silence of the lightning.

Truth does not need a blatant voice,
  or tender thought vehement speech;
  one does not shout, "I love you."

CLINTON LEE SCOTT
PROMISE OF SPRING, 1977

AS WE SPOKE

As we spoke, you and I,
of how the sky at sunset hits the earth
gaily flung notes sounded
of some bird's birding.

  I was that bird in an instant.
  The music fell like fiery drops within my ribcage.
  I felt the tones—
  felt them and yearned—
  and smiled at you and your sunset.

Some day if we trust one another long enough
with care and worth
I'll ask you if you heard that house wren.

   You'd remember.

RUDOLPH W. NEMSER
MOMENTS OF A SPRINGTIME, 1967

PERSEIDS

*The best part of every mind is not that which a person
knows, but that which hovers in gleams, suggestions,
tantalizing before him.*
RALPH WALDO EMERSON

Last August we watched the annual Perseid meteor
shower from a darkened field about twenty miles
south of the city. It was supposed to be an especially
spectacular show that year, but cloud cover prevailed
on the opening night, so we caught the second act
twenty-four hours later, and still managed to see the
streaking blue jet trails igniting the sky.
   Meteor showers are seen best out of the corner of
your eye. The retinas "light detectors" are concen-
trated there. That's also where life's flashes of bril-
liance and radiance generally occur, not directly in

the line of sight, but obliquely, on the borders of conscious awareness.

Meteors descend every night, not in downpours, but in a continuous, gentle rain of heaven misting earthward. if we could retrain our vision we would notice them more often. Ephemeral and incandescent, these celestial visitors remind us that eternity spills and shimmers like quicksilver. Pay attention to what is fleeting, they seem to say. Soften your focus. Adjust your eyes to darkness. Rest your body on the earth. What you are looking for is glimpsed, not seen.

GARY A. KOWALSKI
GREEN MOUNTAIN SPRING, 1997

A COMMON DESTINY

Dedicated to Peg Pierce, January 13, 1974

All living substance, all substance of Energy,
   and Being,
     and Purpose,
are united and share the same destiny.

All people,
   those we love and those we know not of
are united and share the same destiny.

Birth-to-Death
this unity we share with
    the Sun,
    Earth
    our Brothers and Sisters,
    Strangers
    Flowers of the field,
    Snowflakes
    Volcanoes and Moon Beams.

Birth—Life—Death
Unknown—Known—Unknown
Our Destiny: from Unknown to Unknown.

I pray that we will know the Awe
    and not fall into the pit of intellectual arrogance
    in attempting to explain it away.
The Mystery *can* be our substance.
May we have the faith to accept this wonderful Mystery
    and build upon its everlasting Truth.

DAVID H. EATON
BEEN IN THE STORM SO LONG, 1991

THE GROWING SEASON

"I am not religious," says my neighbor, as he hoes the rows between his beans and corn.

"Oh yes, you are," I say to myself.

To plant a seed is an act of faith.
To collect compost is a response of gratitude to the creator.
To water, fertilize, and mulch the ground is an expression of religious responsibility.
To kneel down and pull weeds is a prayer.
To harvest is to participate in the fullness and grace of the spirit.
To protect and replenish creation is to love God.

"I am not religious," says my neighbor.

Yes, you are, I say.

SARA MOORES CAMPBELL
INTO THE WILDERNESS, 1990

GRATITUDE

Often I have felt that I must praise my world
For what my eyes have seen these many years,
And what my heart has loved.
And often I have tried to start my lines:
    "Dear earth," I say,
    And then I pause
    To look once more.
    Soon I am bemused
    And far away in wonder.
So I never get beyond "Dear Earth."

MAX A. KAPP
TO MEET THE ASKING YEARS, 1983

HAWKS

Surely, you too have longed for this—
to pour yourself out
on the rising circles of the air,
to ride, unthinking,
on the flesh of emptiness.

Can you claim, in your civilized life,
that you have never leaned toward
the headlong dive, the snap of bones,

the chance to be so terrible,
so free from evil, beyond choice?

The air that they are riding
is the same breath as your own.
How could you not remember?
That same swift stillness binds
your cells in balance, rushes
through the pulsing circles of your blood.

Each breath proclaims it—
the flash of feathers, the chance to rest
on such a muscled quietness,
to be in that fierce presence,
wholly wind, wholly wild.

LYNN UNGAR
BLESSING THE BREAD, 1996

IT MATTERS

IT MATTERS

I knew a man who had printed on his stationery this proverb: "Nothing is settled. Everything matters." It established a certain ambience for reading his letters, as if to say: what you are about to read is to be taken seriously, but is not final.

I remember him and his proverb sometimes, especially when it seems impossible to change the world or myself in any significant way. Times like the beginnings of new years.

"Sorry, Jim," I say. "It's not true that nothing is settled. In the past year choices have been made, losses have been suffered, there have been growth and decay, there have been commitments and betrayals. None of that can be undone. A year ago no one knew whether during this year one person would become pregnant, another would get cancer, another would take a new job, another would have an accident, but now it is settled.

"One day this year I was present just when someone needed me; another day I was busy doing something else when I was needed. One day I said something to a friend that injured our relationship; another day I said something that enabled a person to see life in a new way. The best and the worst of those days is now written. All my tears, of joy or sorrow, cannot erase it."

If I stay with my meditation long enough, the reply comes. "Robbie," says Jim, "You have misunderstood the proverb. It is true that you cannot escape the consequences of your actions or the chances of the world. But what is not settled is how the story turns out. What is not settled is what the meaning of your life will be."

The meaning of a life is not contained within one act, or one day, or one year. As long as you are alive the story of your life is still being told, and the meaning is still open. As long as there is life in the world, the story of the world is still being told. What is done is done, but *nothing is settled.*

And if nothing is settled, then *everything matters.* Every choice, every act in the new year matters. Every word, every deed is making the meaning of your life and telling the story of the world. Everything matters in the year coming, and, more important, everything matters today.

ROBERT R. WALSH
NOISY STONES, 1992

CIRCLES OF
SELF-ENCAPSULATION

Stifling life into a series of small overlapping circles successfully circumscribes experience and our capacity to respond. People, politics, colors, sounds, pleasures, possibilities, tastes and feelings—what all the circles have in common is that everything within them is known, predictable and organized—and therefore, safe.

The circle of friends includes persons who tend to share our prejudices and enthusiasms, who will be careful of our sensitivities, whose behavior we can predict and accept. Sometimes a friend fails to meet our expectations and is pushed out of the circle. Occasionally someone new passes all our little tests of acceptability and is included in. The circle expands and contracts with changing circumstances, but the goal remains security and sustenance. Who wants to be bothered by people we don't understand, to be challenged by ideas we never knew, to be disturbed by problems we don't know how to solve, to be upset by situations we have no power to correct, to be excited by experiences we are not sure we can control? Who wants to see slums which scar our cities and the scarred persons who live there, or patients who will not recover, or all the other problems that a little generosity and goodwill cannot solve? Who wants to hear about napalm victims or automobile victims or loneliness victims or all the others who have been exploited or crushed in the name of civilization and progress? We can learn to say it so simply: "It's better to be safe than sorry."

It is easier to be safe than alive. Easier to be safe than aware, feeling, responsive, caring, loving, wondering, hoping, joyful and free. It is easier to be safe within the opaque cylinders of self than to risk opening the circles to the dangers of fragmentation. And it is true that we cannot respond to all the stimuli that come pouring in upon us. The attempt to collect experience in quantity is acquisition without meaning. We must be selective in what we permit to enter our consciousness if we are to have any structure in our living.

But I become suspicious about my sacred circles when I am tempted to resent new people, ideas, experiences, perceptions. If we want them all to go away and leave us alone, we are evading life itself.

Paradoxically, the more we seek safety, the more dangers appear, and the more anxious we become. Only as we dare become open to the unexpected and the unknown do we understand how much greater than safety it is to be free.

RICHARD A. KELLAWAY
THE TRYING OUT, 1967

TO OUTGROW THE PAST

To outgrow the past but not extinguish it;
To be progressive but not raw,
Free but not mad, critical but not sterile, expectant
    but not deluded;
To be scientific but not to live on formulas that cut
    us off from life;
To hear amidst clamor the pure, deep tones of the
    spirit;
To seek the wisdom that liberates and a loyalty that
    consecrates;
To turn both prosperity and adversity into servants
    of character;
To master circumstances by the power of principle,
And to conquer death by the splendor of loving
    trust:
This is to attain peace;
This is to pass from drear servitude to divine adoption;
This is to invest the lowliest life with magnificence.
And to prepare it for coronation.

WILLIAM LAURENCE SULLIVAN
IN UNBROKEN LINE, 1974

TRANSCENDING BOUNDARIES

When I was a child, I would stand and gaze at the starry firmament and contemplate infinity. As I stood there, the boundary that is time dissolved; I expanded my Spirit to fill the boundary that is space. My being stilled and all fear, anxiety, and anguish disappeared. Forgotten were the chores, the homework, the ordinary around me.

Transcending boundaries was fun in those days. But, as I reached adulthood, it became more difficult. More and more, the world was with me as I did chores and homework. More and more, my own fears were with me as I encountered others. More and more, I was aware of the boundaries of race, class, age, and sex. I felt myself cringe as the bantering youth in the street came nearer. I felt myself become tearful as I encountered a senior citizen living with pain or the limited choices of a fixed income. I felt myself become angry as I was subjected to the indignities of being rejected by others because I am Black, because I am a woman, or because of the blind person or the openly gay person I was with. I felt myself become unwilling to acknowledge my oneness with the addicted person who is my friend or the homeless people sleeping on the benches in the park.

Today, transcending boundaries is hard work. For one thing, I've created more of them since I was young, and I've built them higher and stronger than they once were. For another thing, I'm much more self-righteous and much less humble than I was then. Sometimes, when I am at my best, I remember that the "other" I distinguish myself from could be me in another time, another place, another circumstance. Then, I remember the words of a colleague who observed that it is "my racism, my sexism, *my* homophobia" that I am called upon to address. So, I take a few deep breaths and begin to release the fears that are the boundaries between me and my fellow humans.

YVONNE SEON
BEEN IN THE STORM SO LONG, 1991

PROPHETS

The best of seers is he who guesses well.
EURIPIDES

Always it is easier to pay homage to prophets
    than to heed the direction of their vision.

It is easier blindly to venerate the saints than to
    learn the human quality of their sainthood.

It is easier to glorify the heroes of the race than
  to give weight to their examples.

To worship the wise, making them gods, is much
  easier than to profit by their wisdom.

Great leaders are honored, not by adulation, but by
  sharing their insights and values.

Grandchildren of those who stoned the prophet
  sometimes gather up the stones
  to build the prophet's monument.

The sky-gods are favored by the enchantment of
  distance, but the earth-gods are victims of
  time exposure.

CLINTON LEE SCOTT
PROMISE OF SPRING, 1977

THE GLOVE IN THE SUBWAY

A one-paragraph newspaper article describes a subway platform during the morning rush hour at
Grand Central Terminal. A train pulls in; a well-
dressed woman gets off. Before the doors close, the
woman realizes that she is holding only one of her
leather gloves. She looks back into the train and

spots the matching one on the seat. It is obviously too late to dash back in to retrieve it, so with a cavalier shrug, she flings her arm out and, the doors about to close, tosses her glove onto the seat alongside its mate. The doors shut, and the train pulls away.

What a great image. One could use it, I suppose, as a metaphor for facing the inevitable, or arguing for an orderly universe, or even, with a little stretch, for sharing the good things in life. But, as we move into the summer season, the metaphor that comes to mind is the one of "letting go."

To throw a favorite leather glove into the oblivion of a moving train must involve small pangs of uncertainty, pangs of some degree of loss, pangs of upset. After a lifetime of struggling not to lose our mittens, then our gloves, cavalier abandonment does not come easy.

In New England at least, our pattern is to cling, as we cling to our gloves, to routine, hard work, and obligation, all fall, all winter, and right through to the Fourth of July. But in the summertime, there is a letting go. We close up our schools and our churches, put our overcoats in moth balls, and dust off the swan boats, the lobster pots and last year's new gas grill. We need that. We need to cast that glove of responsibility back into the train. We need a vigor-

ous and decisive toss about now to free ourselves of
the confining gloves of life, even if we love them.
    And the train's about to leave.

JANE RANNEY RZEPKA
A SMALL HEAVEN, 1989

INCARNATION

I met him in 1962—in Mount Vernon, Iowa.
    He was not a good planner: two hours late for the
        appointment and unaware of the location.
    He was not a commanding presence: short in
        stature and ungainly in movement.
    He was not a handsome figure: slightly overweight
        and clothes too small for the body.
    He was not a congenial person: impatient in
        conversation and never fully present.
    He was not a great speaker: words lost in the nose
        and ill-timed gestures.
    He was not a creative individual: ideas borrowed
        from others and frequent repetition.
    He was not a happy character: wide mournful
        eyes and lips not made for smiling.

But if God appeared anywhere in the 20th
   Century—it was in the form of Martin Luther
   King, Jr.

DAVID O. RANKIN
PORTRAITS FROM THE CROSS, 1978

ON THE ART OF WAITING

How does one learn to wait?

The learning begins with the first drawn breath, the first lusty wail; and it never ceases until the final sigh.

Down the long corridors of confusion, and along the dazzling displays of delight, one tastes of the sounds and fragrances, strives for the definition of the good and the affirmation of the good—the affirmation which brings a way of looking at things, a way which does not change with events.

It comes by representing worthily whatever fates are consigned, keeping well the appointments, knowing that all mankind is us, whether we realize it or not, whether we like it or not. (Beckett)

What are we doing here, that is the question? We seek . . . and we wait.

We would ask it, again and again. Perhaps we get part of an answer: we are not sitting targets for destiny. We are a part of destiny itself.

We are not guilty of the sin of being born; we are blessed with the bounty of life.

This we know, that we are here. Let us meet the needs as we are needed. And whether we are waiting for the dawn to rise or the night to descend, let us keep well our appointments.

CHARLES WHITE McGEHEE
ANSWERS IN THE WIND, 1969

DARK AND LIGHT, LIGHT AND DARK

Blackmail, blacklist, black mark. Black Monday, black mood, black-hearted. Black plague, black mass, black market.

Good guys wear white, bad guys wear black. We fear black cats, and the Dark Continent. But it's okay to tell a white lie, lily-white hands are coveted, it's great to be pure as driven snow. Angels and brides wear white. Devil's food cake is chocolate, angel's food cake is white!

We shape language and we are shaped by it. In our culture, white is esteemed. It is heavenly, sun-

like, clean, pure, immaculate, innocent, and beautiful. At the same time, black if evil, wicked, gloomy,
depressing, angry, sullen. Ascribing negative and
positive values to black and white enhances the insti-
tutionalization of this culture's racism.

Let us acknowledge the negative connotations of
whiteness. White things can be soft, vulnerable, pal-
lid, and ashen. Light can be blinding, bleaching,
enervating. Conversely, we must acknowledge that
darkness has a redemptive character, that in darkness there is power and beauty. The dark nurtured
and protected us before our birth.

Welcome darkness. Don't be afraid of it or deny
it. Darkness brings relief from the blinding sun,
from scorching heat, from exhausting labor. Night
signals permission to rest, to be with our loved ones,
to conceive new life, to search our hearts, to remember our dreams. The dark of winter is a time of
hibernation. Seeds grow in the dark, fertile earth.

The words black and dark don't need to be destroyed or ignored, only balanced and reclaimed in
their wholeness. The words white and light don't
need to be destroyed or ignored, only balanced and
reclaimed in their wholeness. Imagine a world that
had only light—or dark. We need both. Dark and
light. Light and dark.

JACQUI JAMES
BEEN IN THE STORM SO LONG, 1991

ANXIETY

Fill me with anxiety, O Life!
Electrify me, make me nervous
Beyond any staid concern
For those things which challenge
Placid, flaccid ways, anachronisms of being.
Keep me tense, a-tiptoe,
Blinking at the novel,
Reaching out for those things
Just beyond my fingertips;
So that I may make patterns,
Dream dreams, fashion worlds
Which will beat with life.
For I would be a man
And on the move.

ARTHUR GRAHAM
PARTS AND PROPORTIONS, 1961

THIS DAY IS MINE

This day is mine.
May I remember this
and look for something new,
something perhaps I've

stared at all my life
and never seen.

There's music and
there's love and wit and
something that can lift
the mind.

May I discover these
and know the light's
not false and foreign
when I go
toward wonder.

RAYMOND JOHN BAUGHAN
THE SOUND OF SILENCE, 1965

I DO NOT PRAY

I do not pray; but if I did, here is what I would say:
Hear my prayer, O God, my fondest hopes and
    deepest longings:
To hurt as few persons as possible;
To resist the pestilence's of fear, envy, bitterness and
    hate;
To come to terms with disappointment, failure and
    defeat;

To love with all my being:
    with my eyes
    with my hands
    with my heart
To love in every way I can;
To accept the fact that all causes are lost causes, and
    that
there are no victors under the heavens;
To live graciously in a Universe which at best is only
    benignly indifferent to us;
To sometimes experience something other than myself;
To never turn my back to the sun;
To be free enough to celebrate another human being;
To have faith enough, to receive grace enough
    That I may sing,
    Experience Joy,
    Say *Yes* to life even as it destroys me . . .
O God be merciful to us, and help us be merciful to
    ourselves.

JAMES MADISON BARR
73 VOICES, 1972

EACH OF US IS AN ARTIST

Each of us in an artist
Whose task it is to shape life
Into some semblance of the pattern
We dream about. The molding
Is not of self alone, but of shared
Tomorrow and times we shall never see.
So let us be about our task.
The materials are very precious
   and perishable.

ARTHUR GRAHAM
73 VOICES, 1972

GENTLENESS IN LIVING

Be gentle with one another—

It is a cry from the lives of people battered
By thoughtless words and brutal deeds;
It comes from the lips of those who speak them,
And the lives of those who do them.

Who of us can look inside another and know what is
   there
Of hope and hurt, or promise and pain?

Who can know from what far places each has come
Or to what far places each may hope to go?

Our lives are like fragile eggs.
They crack and the substance escapes.
Handle with care!
Handle with exceedingly tender care
For there are human beings within,
Human beings as vulnerable as we are,
Who feel as we feel,
Who hurt as we hurt.

Life is too transient to be cruel with one another;
It is too short for thoughtlessness,
Too brief for hurting.
Life is long enough for caring,
It is lasting enough for sharing,
Precious enough for love.

Be gentle with one another.

RICHARD S. GILBERT
IN THE HOLY QUIET OF THIS HOUR, 1995

MEDITATION ON THE WORD

"In the beginning was the Word . . . ."
In the beginning there is always the word;
   before the action
   can lead to reflection
   there is always the word:

The word of contrition before the act of
   repentance,
The word of forgiveness before the act of
   redemption.

The word of love before the act—
   words formal, halting, half stuck
     in the throat,
   incoherent with meaning—
   words present by their absence

The word of war before the aggression—
   the word deceptive,
     the lie, the cheat and the thrust;
   the word of misery,
     anguished and bloodied
The word of peace before reconciliation—
   allaying the mistrust and anger
   slowing the blood in the veins
   making soft the palpitating temple

bringing hope to people and nations
  that tomorrow will come
  —and they will be alive

"In the beginning was the Word
  and the word was with God . . ."
  and the word made the world of humanity.

PAUL N. CARNES
LONGING OF THE HEART, 1973

ALL THIS TALK OF SAVING SOULS

All this talk of saving souls.
Souls weren't made to save,
like Sunday cloths that
give out at the seams.

They're made for wear; they
come with lifetime guarantees.
Don't save your soul.
Pour it out like rain on
cracked, parched earth.

Give your soul away, or
pass it like a candle flame.
Sing it out, or
laugh it up the wind.

Souls were made for hearing
breaking hearts, for puzzling dreams,
remembering August flowers,
forgetting hurts.

These men who talk of saving souls!
They have the look of bullies
who blow out candles before
you sing happy birthday,
and want the world to be
in alphabetical order.

I will spend my soul,
playing it out like sticky string
into the world,
so I can catch every
last thing I touch.

LINDA M. UNDERWOOD
EXALTATION, 1987

THE MAGICIAN

Once upon a time there was a magician who didn't
know he was one because nobody ever told him he
was, and besides he had been taught from early childhood that magicians were not be taken seriously—
they were trick players, prestidigitating, pretending

to make things happen that can't happen, presuming to have special powers which everybody knows they don't have.

The magician (who didn't know he was) lived simply, minded his own business, and didn't say much and was good to his family and worked at his job as hard as you would expect an ordinary man to work at an ordinary job. When one day he died it was an ordinary sort of death and everybody came to his funeral because Rev. Poke always gave great funeral talks. Rev. Poke began with "swelling prologues to imperial themes" and ended on the same note, swelling.

Some time after the funeral the magician's children discovered a diary which they did not know their father had kept, and they opened it and a jaguar jumped out, and yards and yards of rainbow silk, desperate, beautiful, unwinding.

*For the Spirit searches everything, even the depths of God
For what person knows a man's thoughts except the
spirit of the man which is in Him?*

I CORINTHIANS 2: 10–11

CLARKE WELLS
THE STRANGENESS OF THIS BUSINESS, 1975

TAKE TIME TO LISTEN

There might have been other uses for this moment;
There might have been other pleasures;
There might have been rest,
But there is something beyond all this which I must
    seek.
And except I give it time and attention
It may never come to flower.
It is a yearning for meaning for which the tongue
    has yet no words.
It is a quest for holiness.
It is a quest for self forgiveness,
For all the things wherein I have failed myself
In failing others:
The light I have ignored;
The plea of the spirit, rejected;
The meaning still to be found,
Peace in a world of conflict, and still something more.
It is something only sensed in moments of quiet and
    solitude
Or in the shared meditations of others
Who seek with me.
Perhaps, perhaps it is myself,
Now so buried under the demands and pressures of
    the world

That it may only be found as I take time
To listen for it and to let it grow.

ROBERT T. WESTON
SEASONS OF THE SOUL, 1963

DAY OF PROMISE

DAY OF PROMISE

Here is a day of promise!
May it be so with me, with every one!
The gray clouds scudding overhead,
The stormclouds, rain, and the breaking sunshine,
The apple blossoms bursting in pink and white,
The children gleefully running out to splash in puddles,
The grass green, and the buds
Straining into leaves on shrubs and trees,
And the birds singing, joyfully, in the dawn,
Strutting the lawns as proud possessors.
Everywhere life, life bursting through all fetters,
And the heart singing, protesting against gloom,
Shouting its defiance of clouds and cold;
The gay heart exulting in storm and sunshine alike.
This is a day that aches with the promise of life,
Life which will not be denied.
Let all hearts swell with glad acceptance,
Joyful with the sense of the always becoming,
For out of earth, into the air and sunshine,
    out of ourselves,
There rises spirit in man.
Neither dark nor threat shall thrust it down.
It rises irresistible in us.
This is the season's gift.

ROBERT T. WESTON
SEASONS OF THE SOUL, 1963

NEW YEAR FOR TREES

I share a favorite celebration: Tu Bishvat, the Jewish New Year for Trees. This new year comes midway in the lunar month of Shevat, which rides astride January and February of our solar year. At that time, it is said, the sap begins to rise in the almond trees in Israel.

There is no set service or ritual for Tu Bishvat. It is observed by reading scriptural passages referring to trees, singing seasonal songs, eating fruits and nuts, and—influenced by the American Arbor Day—planting trees. Tu Bishvat is easily adapted to Unitarian Universalist usage.

I was touched by joy when I first discovered Tu Bishvat in a children's book. I have long had a sense of fellowship with trees. Since I was a child, I have sought their company from time to time because I like the way I feel in their presence. I enjoy their beauty, but it is more than that. I used the word "presence" in a very strong sense. I feel their presence as living things. And in that presence, I often feel relaxed and centered, peaceful, restored to inner equilibrium.

For many of us, life is the meaning of the tree. But for me, perhaps the greatest thing about the tree is its silence. Whatever the tree says to us, whatever it answers to our questing, the tree gives its message without words. And the tree bears with us well. It does not judge. It does not react to our anxieties. It does not run after us. It just stands there with open arms.

GRETA W. CROSBY
TREE AND JUBILEE, 1982

PALM SUNDAY

This is what we get in life: We want and want and want—undying love, a world that is fair, eternal life for ourselves and those we care about—and we can't ever have them. We are faced always with a savior dead and gone and an empty tomb to prove it.

We have, I believe, been extended not salvation but mercy. Jesus' "reign of God" is with us—has been with us—radically, mercifully, all along in such forms as kindness, fairness, and wonder. We don't have to wait for Judgment Day, we don't have to be perfect, we don't have to be afraid; we need only look around and awaken to what has existed from the beginning of time.

We go on wanting and hoping and sometimes we are blessed. We don't get what we want—the tomb is still empty. Against that background every act of mercy is cause for rejoicing. One stalk of asparagus,

a kiss, stirring music, a healthy morning, a good
laugh, a kind touch we have all that and all of it, all
of it, is holy.

JANE RANNEY RZEPKA
A SMALL HEAVEN, 1989

PRAYER AT EASTER (FOR A.C.S.)

Lord God of Easter and infrequent Spring,
Thaw our wintry hearts.
Announce the large covenant to deceitful lands,
Drive the sweet liquor through our parched veins.
Stir the vacant eyes with green explosions and gold
    in azure sky.
Smite the pall of death that hangs like desire,
Lure us to fresh schemes of life.
Rouse us from tiredness, self-pity,
Whet us for use,
Fire us with good passion,
Rekindle thy Church.
Restore in us the love of living,
Bind us to fear and hope again.
    As we thank with brief thanksgiving
    Whatever odds may be,
    That life goes on living,
    That the dead rise up ever,

That even the weariest river
Winds back to springs under sea.

For I am the Lord your God,
who stirs up the sea so that its waves roar—
And I have put my words in your mouth,
and hid you in the shadow of my hand,
saying to Zion, "You are my people."
ISAIAH 51:15–16

CLARKE WELLS
THE STRANGENESS OF THIS BUSINESS, 1975

IN SPRING

If I should die (and die I must) please let it be in
    spring
When I, and life up-budding shall be one
And green and lovely things shall blend with all I was
And all I hope to be.
The chemistry
Of miracle within the heart of love and life abundant
Shall be mine, and I shall pluck the star-dust and
    shall know
The mystery within the blade
And sing the wind's song in the softness of the
    flowered glade.

April is the time for parting, not because all nature's
    tears
Presage the blooming time of May
But joyous should be death and its adventure
As the night gives way to day.

GEORGE C. WHITNEY
THE TIDES OF SPRING, 1972

ARBOR DAY

There is a folktale about a young girl who spied an
old man carefully planting trees in an orchard:
apple, pear, and cherry. He was stooped with age,
and she looked at him with puzzlement. "Why are
you planting those?" she asked finally. "You may not
live long enough to enjoy the fruit when the trees
finally begin to bear."

"That's true," the old man replied calmly. "But
when I was born, there were trees here for me to
enjoy that I did not plant. Now it is my turn to do
something for future generations."

There are many ways to make a lasting contribu-
tion to the world. Planting a tree is only one. Some
work for peace, others volunteer to tutor children

after school or work at the local animal shelter. The important thing is to give your energies to something bigger than your own ego, something that can outlast your own lifetime.

Each of us can truly say, "I have harvested where I did not sow." And so we should give something back to the world—not "should" in any moralistic sense, but in the same manner that acorns should produce oak trees and apple seeds should make pippins. Gratitude is a natural outgrowth of living, service a response to the abundance with which we have been blessed.

Henry David Thoreau wrote, "Though I do not believe that a plant will spring up where no seed has been, I have great faith in a seed. Convince me that you have a seed there, and I am prepared to expect wonders."

GARY A. KOWALSKI
GREEN MOUNTAIN SPRING, 1997

MOTHER'S DAY

Your children are not your children.
They are the sons and daughters of Life's longing for itself.

They come through you but not from you,
And though they are with you yet they belong not to you.
—KAHLIL GIBRAN

Though my child belongs not to me, she is my child and always will be.

I watched her running up the driveway on that second day of school, bouncing along in white ankle socks and Stride Rite sandals and a summer dress hand-sewn by an English grandma. I watched her at eight and nine, two yellow braids and a Cookie Monster lunch box. I dropped what I was doing and ran out to meet the bus, in those days when she was little enough to be swept up in my arms and unembarrassed by my affection.

I watched her carrying a trombone case and a school bag that just gets heavier, trudging up that driveway on cold winter mornings in junior high when no one wore a winter jacket or socks, no matter how much snow covered the yard. I watched her just last week when her boyfriend came to meet her in his car, and they walked out together arm in arm, he carrying the trombone case. Then, when I watched her asking questions of the admissions officer at a liberal arts college, I knew that I could count the number of days I have left to watch her from the window.

Spirit of life, watch my child when I cannot. Encircle her with love, protect her from a world which

has become cynical. Knowing that I cannot stop
time, not even for a moment, and freeze the picture
of her from my window, let me hold her gently in
my memory. Let all those children she once was
remain joyful spirits enriching my reminiscences.
Spirit of life, watch all our children. Keep them safe
as they adventure toward adulthood, and let them
turn and wave to us as they step out of our care and
into the world of their making.

ELIZABETH TARBOX
LIFE TIDES, 1993

GIVE THANKS

Give thanks, give thanks
all life is this
   what shall our thanks be?
   how shall we frame them?
     love and laughter
     ready smiles
     joy in the heart
   to make our thanks live,
   how shall we shape them?
     gentle touch
     steady voice
     persistent step.

whom shall we thank?
who is it we seek?
   God and Allah
   Jehovah, sun
   cloud and rain
   and one another.

LIBBIE STODDARD
STOPPING PLACES, 1974

WHEN GIVING THANKS COMES HARD

When giving thanks comes hard for you,
And things are grim,
   And hope runs thin,
      Recall:
Despair's a door to pass on through,
   And not a home for living in.
When thanksgiving fills your cup,
And those you love are all about,
Look at your blessings, count them up,
and give back something to the world
without.

Go in peace.
Go *for* peace.

For all who see God,
May God go with you.

For all who embrace life,
May life return your affection.

For all who seek a right path,
May a way be found . . .

And the courage to take it
Step by step.
Amen.

ROBERT MABRY DOSS
EXALTATION, 1987

AUTUMNAL INVITATION

Dark, dank, moss-covered stones of autumn. Layer
upon layer of moldering leaves, decomposing, separating molecules, changing, becoming earth.

There is a fearfulness which infects the fantasies
of a lone walker through these leaves, sinking
through the season of decay, feeling the inevitability
of that invitation to return to the earth. The rain
soaks through me, dripping off the trees above,
washing me away, back into the fullness of nature's
womb. Come, she invites, lie down, rest in me,
return to me. Come back.

But life is the interval when we rise up and move against the margin of air, earth, and water. Life is the slow drawing together of our moisture-dipped cells so we can surge with the wind and press against the great sky. I shall walk on for a while yet, stretching toward the stars of my dreams, resisting the pull of the earth while I can still breathe. For there is work to do for human beings, there is love to make, poems to write, and nights of dancing to the moon. There are calls to answer and songs yet to sing, and the earth will wait. She will wait; we will be there soon enough.

ELIZABETH TARBOX
LIFE TIDES, 1993

IMPORTANT NOTICE

The newsletter editor of the First Parish in Wayland, Massachusetts, recently ran her favorite *New Yorker* squib:

"IMPORTANT NOTICE. If you are one of the hundreds of parachuting enthusiasts who bought our *Easy Sky Diving* book, please make the following correction: On page 8, line 7, the words 'state zip code' should have read 'pull rip cord.' —Adv. in the Warrenton, (Va.) Fauquier Democrat."

I worry about things like this during the Christmas season. Had I been a parachuting enthusiast, and had I breezed through *Easy Sky Diving* during the month of December, I'd still be flying through the air, picking up speed, shouting my zip code.

Zip codes aren't important. Rip cords are. During the Advent season, it's all too easy to confuse one for the other. The "zip codes" of the season—the replacement bulbs, the four sticks of butter, the fruit-by-mail catalogs, the party shoes—have our attention, and before we know it, we're picking up speed and shouting out those "zip codes" without ever asking why.

Perhaps we should look to our rip cords. Our lifelines, in December as always, are our inner quiet, the love we exchange, and our efforts to make the world more whole. We can slow the descent. We can take in the view. And we can anticipate a gentle landing on the twenty-fifth.

JANE RANNEY RZEPKA
A SMALL HEAVEN, 1989

ALL I WANT FOR CHRISTMAS

This is a time of year when we ask—and are asked—what do you want? Shall it be another tie, a new pair of gloves, a book? We ask and we answer. We shop, we wrap, we ship. And the season usually comes and goes without us ever really answering the question: *What do you want?*

Some of the things we want we might be afraid to ask for because we can't be sure what we would do if we got them. Many things we want we don't know enough to ask for. Most things we can't ask for because we know no one can give them to us.

Most people ask the question without any interest in really knowing, yet it can be a question for each of us to hold on to for a time in mind and heart. What do we want? Not what would we like, but what do we want to give us a deeper connection with life and to help us give expression to our love? Not a long list of things, but a sense of clarity that illuminates what it is we are doing and why. Not outward signs of generosity, but an internal sense of caring that guides us to give in any season. Not just the reflex of always giving, but also the courage to truly answer some of those people who ask us, "What do you want?"

Dare to answer. Think of the things you want, and the things that others close to you would want. Imagine the ways they might be given and received.

What do you want?

DAVID S. BLANCHARD
A TEMPORARY STATE OF GRACE, 1997

IN OUR PRACTICED PESSIMISM

O God, in our practiced pessimism it is difficult to be less than cynical about Christmas. We too have followed stars but they never led us to Bethlehem. We have known many wise ones whose wisdom faded when tested by our experience. Angel voices for us usually turn out to be singing commercials. Words of peace are used to defend acts of aggression. Herod and Caesar still reign. The world as created is not as we would have it. And yet, and yet . . . .

Somewhere a child just drew its first breath and the parents share in the primal joy of Christmas. A child estranged from its parents has decided to call home and the sound of his voice will bring the hope of reconciliation. Someone has given a gift where there was no expectation of giving or receiving. An aged person, ill and unloved, has just found mercy in the mantle of death.

O God, it's not your world, it's ours. Give us the courage to accept it, the grace to embrace it, the will to love it. Enable us, we pray, to appreciate and expand the moments of joy in life, whenever they come. Let them be for us bearers of hope which will enable us to endure any hour of despair, to the end that we, while the gift of life is ours, may help push back the dark with the flame of our faith.

PAUL N. CARNES
LONGING OF THE HEART, 1973